EDGAR'S WALKING GUIDES

HAUNTED LONDON

Copyright © Edgar's Guides Ltd, 2020

All rights reserved. No part of this book may be reprinted or reproduced or utilised in any form or by any electronic, mechanical or other means, now known or hereafter invented, including photocopying and recording, or in any information storage or retrieval system, without the prior permission in writing of the publishers.

All images publisher's own unless stated. Contemporary newspaper illustrations courtesy the British Library Board.

ISBN 978-1-8382342-3-2

Published by Edgar's Guides Ltd
71-75 Shelton Street, London WC2H 9JQ

Peruse the full catalogue,
access video clips and download free extras at
www.EdgarsGuides.com

No. 4

HAUNTED LONDON

EDGAR SAYS

"There's something utterly thrilling about conducting one's own tour of history as you perambulate the thoroughfares, away from the crowds, able to pause on a whim to savour the moment. Allow me to be your companion as I guide you to some of my favourite places, from the well-known to the obscure, and suggest some of my preferred establishments for refreshment along the way. My thanks to my chums Mr. Richard Jones and Mr. Adam Wood for mapping out this excursion."

SAFETY NOTICE

Please be sure to be careful as you walk the route. Stay familiar with your surroundings at all times, and take particular care when you are crossing roads. Every effort has been made to ensure that the directions are accurate, but obviously, things can change and mistakes can be made, so the publishers cannot be held responsible for errors or their consequences. In the current Covid-aware times there are sanitising pots at Underground stations, which we recommend using before setting out. Please also be aware that some parts of the route may require the wearing of face masks, so ensure you have one with you at all times. Other than that, enjoy the walk and I hope it brings you as much joy as it did me when I encountered the wonderful places that you will be visiting.

I

*In screaming woods and empty rooms
or gloomy vaults and sunken tombs;
Where monks and nuns in dust decay
and shadows dance at close of day.*

II

*Where the bat dips on the wing
and spectral choirs on breezes sing;
Where swords of ancient battles clash
and shimmering shades for freedom dash.*

III

*Where raging storms at midnight howl
and distant rolls of thunder growl.
Where the hounds of hell take flight
and ghost clouds race across the night.*

IV

*Where silver webs of spiders weave
and star-crossed lovers take their leave.
Where curses lay the spirits low
and mortal footsteps fear to go.*

V

*Where death holds life in grim embrace
its lines etched on the sinner's face.
Where e'er the march of time is flaunted
voices cry - "this place is haunted."*

© (1999) Richard Jones
All rights reserved.

HAUNTED LONDON

Do you believe in ghosts? Have you ever seen a ghost? I only ask because, in the pages that follow, you will be able to embark upon two journeys through the streets of haunted London, and, given the fact that you are going to visit 40 locations where ghosts have been seen, well, shall we just say that if you believe in them, they might come!

Of course, not everybody believes in ghosts, nor should they. Dr Margarete Murray, the president of the Folklore Society in the 1950s, certainly was no believer, as can be gleaned from her address to the Society given on the 8th of March 1954. "Belief in ghosts," she told the assembled members, "like belief in the Devil, is dying out."

She then went on to reason ghosts are notoriously fond of darkness:

"...but now every town and most villages have street lamps, houses are lighted by electricity, vehicles have headlamps which illuminate the dark lane, and pedestrians no longer carry a lantern with a flickering rush light, but can flash the ray of an electric torch on

any uncanny-looking object they see – or think they see..."

As it transpires, Dr Murray's sentiments have turned out to be not at all prophetic. Indeed, interest in ghosts has increased dramatically over the last twenty or so years, and people love to experience haunted locations first-hand on organised ghost hunts, or even just with groups of friends or family.

And where better to search for supernatural entities than around the streets of London?

London has the reputation of being the most haunted capital city in the world, with ghosts that span the centuries and often illuminate dark corners of a brutal past. From those who perished inside England's most haunted building, the Tower of London, to the tragic victims of the world's most famous serial killer, Jack the Ripper, many of the phantoms that roam the capital are an essential part of British history, folklore and legend.

London originated with the Romans, and since their departure from these shores, nigh on 1,600 years ago, centuries of demolition and rebuilding have seen the level of its streets rise by an amazing 28 feet.

Millions of people have lived and died here, and in consequence, there is not one square inch of the old city that is not imbued with the memories and experiences of these former citizens.

There is an old saying that ghosts only ever appear in places that have known either great happiness or great misery, and the buildings and streets of London have certainly known both in abundance.

But what exactly are these 'things' that we call ghosts?

The most frequent question I get asked as I go about my business, collecting and researching ghost stories and hauntings, is, "Do you believe in ghosts?"

The answer to that question has to be an emphatic "Yes." There have, over the centuries, been too many accounts of ghosts and hauntings from honest, reliable and publicity-shy people for them not to exist.

I certainly do not believe that they are the dead coming back to haunt the living; indeed, the more I research and explore supernatural phenomenon – and over the past forty years I have travelled the length and breadth of Britain and Ireland, visiting close on 4,000 haunted places – the more I become convinced that ghosts are little more than strong emotions that have somehow become imprinted upon their surroundings, and there are certain people who are more attuned to these 'recordings' than the rest of us. This may be why ghosts can be so personal. You might have an entire group of people present when a haunting occurs, and yet only a tiny minority of them might be lucky – or unlucky – enough to see the ghost.

Hauntings, of course, can assume many different forms.

It is, in fact, very rare for people to actually 'see' a ghost. People sense them, smell them, feel them and hear them, but a full-blown manifestation tends to be the exception rather than the rule.

In recent years, largely since the advent of digital cameras, there has been a sharp increase in the number of supposed ghost photographs, mostly consisting of so-called 'orbs'.

These floating balls of circular light are one of the most common types of alleged paranormal activity. Believers enthusiastically hail them as spirit manifestations, and it has been theorised that they may be a type of spirit energy that is not normally visible to the naked eye, but which can be captured on camera. Some believe them to be spirits that have willingly stayed behind because they feel bound to their previous life or previous location.

One enthusiastic orbist even goes as far as to declare them to be "multi-dimensional beings", and claims that some of them are "...currently being used by Inter-planetary life forms to view life on Earth and other planets."

Personally, I am very dubious about orbs and

think there is nothing in the least bit ghostly about the majority of them. As my friend John Mason – a professional photographer who is, seemingly, forever on the road taking infra-red, ordinary film and digital images of thousands of haunted places – points out, orbs are mostly a product of the digital age. He believes them to be nothing more than light reflecting off particles of dust or moisture in the atmosphere; in other words, physical rather than psychical.

But ghost stories are as popular now as ever they were in the past, and in the pages that follow you will find a guide to some great locations where decidedly odd things have been known to occur.

Some of the stories are well known and have been handed down through the ages and, no doubt, have been embellished with each retelling! After all, let's be honest about this, there is nothing better than a ghostly tale told at a spooky location in hushed and reverential tones. I can feel the hairs standing up on the back of my neck even as I write these words!

Although I have tried, wherever possible, to offer historical corroboration for the events that led to some of the hauntings, I have set the stories down, more or less, as they have been recounted by those who have experienced them. I have made little attempt to explain *why* they happen, but have, instead, remained content to just accept that they *do* happen.

As you make your way around the routes, take your time, savour your surroundings, and linger for as long as time or courage will allow at those locations that you find charged with paranormal energy.

And, it should it happen that you chance upon a ghost, or two, or three – then I would be delighted to hear of your experience!

Edgar

PART ONE: THE HAUNTED CITY

Map on inner front cover

Start: Barbican Underground Station

End: The Blackfriars public house,
174 Queen Victoria Street EC4V 4EG

Duration: 2 hours

Best of Times: Evenings

The City of London is, well... it's just special. 2,000 years of history crackle away in its streets, and vestiges of the past are all around you. It has experienced highs and lows. It has been burned, bombed, razed and rebuilt. In short, it is a survivor.

Since its founding by the Romans, 2,000 years ago, the City has seen an amazing array of happenings. Tragedies and disasters aplenty have afflicted it. But there have also many glories, and if there is one thing the City of London knows how to do with aplomb, it is celebrate.

It is inevitable that, with so much history, that some of the bygone residents should still return to enjoy the places that they knew so well in life, and on this walk you are going to twist and turn through a warren of alleyways and streets that snake their way from Barbican, in the north of the City, to Blackfriars in the south.

You're are going to visit old buildings that managed to dodge the flames of the Great Fire of London. You will visit a plague pit and an execution ground, both of which are haunted. You will be able to dip into timeless pubs to enjoy a beverage, and to try and contact the spirits of former landlords or patrons that have left their mark upon the ethereal fabric of the buildings. But you are also going to see a completely different side of the City of London than most casual visitors get to see.

So, get those walking shoes ready, and let's set off on a special and spectral journey through the haunted hinterland of the City of London.

HIGHLIGHTS OF THE HAUNTED CITY WALK

Here are some of the chill-inducing highlights you will encounter as you make your way through the thoroughfares of the ghostly City of London:

- A 14th century plague pit, from which the moans and groans of those buried there are said to emanate in the dead of night.

- The 'holy gloom' of London's oldest parish church, the walls of which drip with atmosphere and where a ghostly monk keeps a weary vigil.

- The infamous location where the 'Fires of Smithfield" blazed during the religious persecutions of the 16th century, where agonised screams are carried on the night breezes.

- The most haunted pub in the City of London, inside which it is possible to descend into the creepy cellars to look for the spirits that lurk down there!

- The dark court where the fearsome phantom of the Black Dog of Newgate has been known to chill the blood of many a late-night wanderer.

- An ancient bell that tolls whenever... well, read on to find for whom, and why, it tolls.

> *To begin, turn left out of Barbican Underground Station and go first left along Carthusian Street. A little way along on the right you will find*

1. THE SUTTON ARMS

There is no doubt about it, the Sutton Arms is as snug a hostelry as you could ever wish to encounter in this world – or the next. Indeed, it would appear to be a popular resort for at least one 'other-worldly' visitor who seems unable to resist the urge to return to this enchanting bow-windowed pub, where he has been known to startle the occasional patron.

Nobody knows for certain who he is, or was, other than successive landlords have come to know him as 'Charley.'

'Charley' is a red-haired gentleman of advanced years who seems content to just sit in a favoured corner of the pub, simply watching the toings-and-froings of daily life around him – although quite which era's toings-and-froings he is actually watching is a matter of some conjecture.

He once startled two ladies, who were enjoying a lunchtime drink in the Sutton arms, by appearing alongside them, and then abruptly disappearing again.

On another occasion, a friend of the then landlord, who was staying in an upstairs room, was combing her hair in the mirror, when she caught the reflection of a red-haired old man standing behind her, smiling. Affronted by the uninvited guest, she turned to remonstrate with him, only to find that, other than herself, the room was empty.

Continue along Carthusian Street, and go right into the gates of the grassed garden which is

2. CHARTERHOUSE SQUARE

Many people consider this to be one of the neighbourhood's most melancholic spots. The huge plane trees that tower above the peaceful lawns stand over a plague pit where 50,000 victims of the 1348 Black Death are said to be buried. Some of them would, no doubt, have been buried alive, and people walking by the square during the hours of darkness can sometimes hear the anguished screams of these poor unfortunates as they relive their final agonies amid the putrefying corpses.

When the Charterhouse School stood nearby, new

Edgar's Guide To...

Charterhouse Square

pupils were dared to creep into the square as midnight approached, press an ear to the cold earth and, as the witching hour chimed, listen to the screeching and howling that they were assured would sound from beneath the grass.

....

☞ *Walk diagonally left across the square to exit via the gate on the other side (of the garden), and cross to the huge wooden gates that are the entrance to the Charterhouse itself.*

....

3. THE CHARTERHOUSE

The ancient wall of weathered stone that encircles the Charterhouse – London's only surviving Tudor town house – helps keep the contemporary world firmly at bay.

Beyond the massive oak gates of the gatehouse, visitors find themselves in a veritable time capsule, the origins of which stretch back to 1381 when Norman nobleman Sir Walter Manny endowed a monastery for the strict order of the Carthusian monks. Here the holy brethren would offer prayers for the souls of the victims of the 1348 Black Death, who still lie buried in the great square outside the gates. The monastery flourished until the Reformation, when its monks refused to accept Henry VIII as head of the church in England.

Their Prior, John Houghton, was hanged, drawn and quartered, and one of his arms was even nailed onto the monastery gates in attempt to persuade the surviving monks. But, inspired by their leader's bravery and ghostly nocturnal visits from long-dead members of their order, who urged them to remain true to their faith, the friars held strong and refused to curtail to the King's demands.

One dark, wintry night, as they prayed in the chapel by dim candlelight, there came a flash of heavenly flame which caused every candle to flare up with a celestial brilliance. Encouraged in their battle with the State, the monks remained steadfast, even though sixteen more of their number were executed before the monastery was finally dissolved.

The building was then granted to Lord North, who turned it into a splendid private residence. He entertained Elizabeth I here on two occasions, his hospitality being so lavish that he crippled himself financially and had to retire to the country.

Thomas Howard, 4th Duke of Norfolk, then bought the house. His plans to marry Mary, Queen of Scots, resulted in his execution in 1572, and the house had several more owners before being purchased in 1611 by the immensely wealthy Sir Thomas Sutton. He converted he building into a hospital for aged men and a school for the education of the sons of the poor. In time the school became a distinguished public school, and moved to new premises in Godalming in 1867.

Today, some twenty or so elderly men live amid the ancient courts and forgotten cloister of this wonderful old mansion.

At night, when the surrounding streets fall silent,

Entrance to the Charterhouse

a shadowy monk is said to drift aimlessly about the cobblestone courtyards, parts of which survive from the days of the monastery. He shares his weary vigils with the headless spectre of the Duke of Norfolk that comes striding down the main staircase, on which he was arrested, his head tucked neatly under his arm.

Facing the gates, go left, and walk along the cobblestoned road to exit via the gates ahead. Go first left into Fox and Knot Street, veer right and make your way along Lindsay Street, turning left along Long Lane, then go over the crossing, and turn right down the covered passageway to the left of Ye Old Red Cow. On arrival at the other side, pause and look up at the first floor window.

4. YE OLDE RED COW

This pub was, for many years, under the tenancy of Dick O'Shea, a characterful Irishman who attracted the likes of Bernard Miles and Peter Ustinov to try his legendary hot whisky toddies.

The pub was open from 6.30am, serving the workers after their nightly duties at Smithfield Market, opposite. Once the pub was open, Dick would sit in his rocking chair by this window keeping an eye on his customers below.

He died in 1981 but, for almost a year afterwards, regulars often caught sight of him, sitting on the balcony, rocking back and forth in this window, as genial and watchful a host in death as he had been in life.

 Turn right along Cloth Fair, and on arrival at the Rising Sun, go right along Rising Sun Court beside

it, then turn right just after the pub to squeeze into the delightfully-spooky little passage, where, a little way along on the right, are what appear to be the remains of gravestones against the wall. You can either linger in the passage for this story, or, better still, go inside the pub for a libation.

....

5. THE RISING SUN

This cosy and traditional 18th century hostelry lay derelict and empty for much of the 20th century until,

Edgar's Guide To...

in 1984, Tadcaster brewer Samuel Smith purchased and refurbished the building. Its proximity to St Bartholomew's Hospital has led to a local tradition that, in the early 19th century, a gang of bodysnatchers used the pub as a meeting place, and later as a hunting ground for cadavers with which to supply the research needs of doctors.

Whether there is any truth in the rumour that this dastardly band would replenish their merchandise by drugging and murdering patrons of the Rising Sun is debatable. But what is certain is that some long-ago act of infamy has left a psychic stain upon the pub's ethereal plane, and managers and staff have, over the years, encountered several ghosts.

Two Brazilian barmaids who worked here in 1989, and lived in, would often be woken in the early hours, by a 'presence' that would sit on the end of their beds, and which would, occasionally, slowly tug the bed clothes off them. Several barmen who have been cleaning up in the downstairs bar late at night have been disturbed by the distinct sounds of footsteps running across the floor of the upstairs bar. However, when they went to investigate, the room was always empty.

Finally, in 1990, the then landlady was enjoying a shower in the staff bathroom one summer's afternoon when she thought she heard the bathroom door open and close. The next moment the shower curtain was pulled slowly aside, and an ice-cold hand ran down her back. She turned quickly, but found that she was alone.

....

From the Rising Sun, cross Cloth Fair and enter the churchyard via the iron gate. The church that towers over you is

....

6. THE PRIORY CHURCH OF ST BARTHOLOMEW THE GREAT

This is the oldest parish church in London. It possesses a dark and mysterious interior, the ancient walls of which drip with atmosphere and which make a wonderful spot for ghost hunters to soak in the true ambience of historic and haunted London.

It has been used as a location for films as diverse as *Robin Hood, Prince of Thieves* and *Four Weddings and a Funeral*. Its ambience has been described as the 'holy gloom', and it comes as little surprise to learn that the building is haunted.

Even its beginnings are tinged with the supernatural. Rahere, a man who, according to legend, was once a jester at the court of King Henry I, founded it in 1123.

In November 1120, the King's only son and heir had been drowned when the White Ship was lost in a winter storm off Calais. The court was plunged into despondency, and Rahere opted to become a monk and set off on a pilgrimage to Rome. Whilst there he fell dangerously ill with malaria, and on his death bed vowed that if he were cured and allowed to return to his own country, he would 'erect a hospital for the restoration of poor men.'

Miraculously, Rahere's prayer was answered, and he duly set off for England. But on the way he had

a terrible dream in which he was seized by a fearful winged creature and taken up onto a high ledge, where he was set down, teetering on the brink of a yawning chasm. Just as he was about to fall, the radiant figure of St Bartholomew appeared at his side, and told Rahere that he had come to save him. In return, said the saint, "in my name thou shalt found a church... in London, at Smedfeld [Smithfield]."

Thus the church was founded, and when he died in 1145, Rahere was buried inside.

His tomb now stands to the left of the altar, its reverse

Rahere's tomb

side clearly showing the results of a hasty repair carried out in the 19th century when the parish officials decided to report upon the state of the founder's body. It was well preserved, and even the clothes and sandals were said to have been intact. A few days after the tomb had been sealed, one of the church officers fell ill and confessed that, when the tomb had been open, he had stolen one of the sandals. He gave it back and recovered, but it was never returned to the foot of its rightful owner, and since that day Rahere has haunted the church as a shadowy, hooded figure that appears from the gloom, brushes past astonished witnesses, and fades slowly into thin air.

On other occasions his appearances have been more active. In the mid 20th century, the Reverend W.F.G. Sandwich was showing two ladies around the church, when he sighted a monk standing in the pulpit, giving a very animated sermon to an unseen congregation, although no sound could be heard. The two ladies appeared to be oblivious to the apparition, but just to be sure, the Reverend Sandwich directed their attention to the pulpit, making the observation, "I don't think that pulpit is worthy of the church, do

The interior of St Bartholomew the Great

you?" The ladies merely agreed with him, obviously quite unaware of the ghostly monk.

In May 1999, the then verger of the church, John Caster, who lived in the house next door, was woken early one morning by a telephone call from the security company, informing him that the alarms were going off inside the church. Entering the building, he turned on the lights and conducted a brief search. The church was empty. Switching the lights off, he was about to leave when he clearly heard the measured tread of slapping footsteps, walking down the central aisle. He called out, "Who's there?", whereupon the footsteps stopped for a moment. But then they resumed continued along the aisle. Convinced there was an intruder, he locked the doors and called the police. They arrived within minutes, but could find no sign of anyone inside the building. Furthermore, no windows or doors were open.

The next morning the alarm company sent an engineer to check and reset the motion triggered alarms. Both he and John were astonished to discover that only the central beam, the one that passes Rahere's tomb, had been broken. The beams by the doors, and the side and top aisles, had not been breached, meaning that whatever – or whoever – was responsible, had somehow managed to simply 'appear' at the centre of the church.

It was then that John remembered that the footsteps had sounded like sandals, slapping over the stone floor of the old church.

....

> *Cross the churchyard and go down the steps in the far corner. Turn right, and exit via the lovely gatehouse. Keep ahead, and pause on the left by the plaque on the wall to Sir William Wallace.*

....

7. THE FIRES OF SMITHFIELD

The 'Smoothfield', as Smithfield was originally known, was for many years one of London's places of execution. In August 1305, Sir William Wallace, Braveheart, was put to death here, and a grey granite plaque on the wall of St Bartholomew's Hospital still commemorates his heroic exploits.

He is not one, however, of the ghosts that haunt the spot where his life was ended all those centuries ago. The ghosts of Smithfield belong to a later reign, when Mary Tudor attempted to restore England to the Catholic faith and chose to do it using fire and the sword.

In the reign of Queen Mary Tudor, over two hundred Protestants were put to death in England, and many of them were burnt at Smithfield. 'Bloody Mary' was emphatic that green wood should not be used, since its smoke was likely to suffocate the victims before they suffered the full agony of the flames.

We can only guess at the terrible suffering endured by those who perished here, as Mary strove to undo the work of her father, Henry VIII, and her brother, Edward VI, and bring Catholicism back to the people of England. For some of her victims the torment appears to have proved eternal, and those who work in the area in the early hours of the morning have often been disturbed by anguished and agonised screams that rend the air, and by the sickly smell of burning flesh that is carried upon the night breezes.

☞ *Keep ahead, noticing how the wall on your left has a large amount of damage. This is, in fact, shrapnel damage from the First World War when a Zeppelin airship dropped a bomb on the square. A little further along, pause on the left and look up at the magnificent gatehouse of St Bartholomew's Hospital, where in a niche above the arch you can admire the*

only outdoor statue of Henry VIII in London.

8. THE HENRY VIII GATEHOUSE

Henry VIII's is not a name that you would readily associate with healing the sick and saving lives. Indeed, quite the opposite is likely to be your first thought when you think of the six-times married monarch, whose contribution to surgical science consisted, in most people's minds, of the 'separating of heads from their bodies' variety.

Yet, it is to Henry that London owes the survival of its oldest hospital, the hospital of St Bartholomew, or 'Bart's' as it has been affectionately known to generations of Londoners.

Founded in 1123, the hospital developed a good reputation for, if not always actually curing the sick, then certainly for making their afflictions that little bit more bearable.

Patients were nursed, given rest and comfort, plus a reasonable amount of food, together with a goodly amount of ale, and when – or if – a patient was discharged, they would be sent on their way with a nice pair of new shoes that had been crafted in the monastery's own tannery.

And then, in 1534, Henry VIII went and almost

ruined it all by declaring himself Supreme Head of the Church in England and setting in motion the Dissolution of the Monasteries.

The Priory of St Bartholomew was suppressed in 1539, and the hospital would, no doubt, have followed suit had not the City fathers panicked at the prospect of all the poor that the hospital had succeeded in keeping hidden from their view over the preceding centuries suddenly become an all-too visible fixture of everyday City of London life.

Thus, they petitioned Henry, asking that he grant the hospital back to the City on account of the fact it was urgently needed to help "the myserable people lyeng in the streete, offendyng every clene person passyng by the way with theyre fylthye and nastye savors."

It took a bit more appealing to Henry's extremely well-hidden caring and considerate side, not to mention a few false starts, before, on 27th December 1546, he finally granted the "Hospital formally known as St Bartholomew's" to the City of London. However, he was most insistent that the name be changed to the far catchier "House of the Poore in West Smithfield in the suburbs of the City of London, of King Henry VIII's foundation."

Officially speaking, this remained the hospital's actual name until 1948, although generations of Londoners chose to ignore such a grandiose-sounding title in favour of just plain Bart's!

Still, Henry had done right by the hospital, so the hospital felt duty bound to do right by Henry – albeit it took them almost two hundred years to show their appreciation.

In 1701, the hospital's governors decided that the north gate should be rebuilt and, in 1702, they agreed to pay John Strong, Junior Mason – and a member of the Strong family of Masons who, at the time, were labouring away at rebuilding nearby St Paul's Cathedral with Sir Christopher Wren – the princely sum of £550 to erect for them a splendid new gatehouse.

And, over the arch, they placed a statue of Henry VIII, the despotic King who, for all his faults, was responsible for ensuring that the hospital survived his break with Rome and could continue to administer to the sick of London.

It has performed its service to generations of Londoners ever since, and is still going strong.

....

☞ *Go in through the gate, keep ahead through the covered roadway that passes beneath the hospital's Great Hall, and pause in the lovely square.*

....

9. ST BARTHOLOMEW'S HOSPITAL

St Bartholomew's Hospital has the distinction of being the oldest hospital in London to still stand on its original site. It's origins stretch back to 1123, when it was founded, as we have heard, as part of the monastery of St Bartholomew by Rahere, a court jester turned man of God.

In the depths of the hospital there is a elevator, which generations of doctors and nurses have come to know as the 'coffin lift'. In the silent hours of early mornings, it has been known to take bemused passengers down

to the basement, irrespective of which floor they have pressed for. Once there, its lights go out and it will not move. After a few moments of madly pushing the buttons, staff will pull open the gates and walk back to the ground floor. Here they find the lift waiting, its gates open and its lights on. Should they then choose to walk up to the required level, they suffer the unnerving experience of having the elevator follow them up the lift shaft, around which the staircase twists.

Tradition maintains that the ghost of a nurse, who was once murdered in the lift in the basement by a deranged patient, is responsible for the malfunction.

The spirits of former nurses also haunt other parts

of the hospital. Grace Ward is the spectral domain of the Grey Lady, a nurse in old-fashioned uniform who, in life, is said to have administered a fatal overdose to a patient and to have killed herself in remorse. Now, whenever nurses are about to make a similar mistake, they are said to feel a light tap on their shoulders and, looking up, they see the grey lady, shaking her head in warning.

A similarly-attired lady has been seen on Bedford Fenwick Ward, although she appears to administer comfort. Nurses have long grown used to patients, shortly before they die, asking them to thank the old-fashioned nurse for bringing them a cup of tea.

....

Backtrack to the Henry VIII Gate, go left along Giltspur Street, cross to its right side, and pause on the next corner, Cock Lane. Be sure to look up at

....

10. THE GOLDEN BOY OF PYE CORNER

He marks the spot where the Great Fire of London burn itself out in 1666. With most of their City destroyed, Londoners sought a supernatural reason for the devastation, and they found it here at was then known as Pye Corner. They reasoned that, since the fire (it wasn't so 'great' initially) had begun at Pudding

Edgar's Guide To...

Lane and, in this quarter of the City, had ended at Pye Corner, it was a clear sign from God that they had been punished for the sin of gluttony. And, so, to enforce the moral, they put this rotund cherub up on the wall to commemorate that punishment.

11. THE COCK LANE GHOST

Cock Lane is now a relatively uninteresting thoroughfare, whose chief glory is the cherubic fat boy that is perched high up on its north-eastern side to mark the spot where the Great Fire of London burnt itself out.

Number 33 was long ago demolished, which is a great pity, for in the late 18th century one of London's most infamous hauntings occurred there, at what was then the home of William Parsons.

One morning in 1760, Parsons offered lodgings to a widower named William Kent. Kent gratefully accepted, and moved in with his sister-in-law, Miss Fanny, with whom he had become romantically involved. Not long after the two lovers had taken up residence, Parson's borrowed a considerable sum of money from Kent, and showed a marked reluctance to repay it.

With relations strained between the two men, Kent was suddenly called away on business and Miss Fanny, rather than sleep alone, took Parsons' eleven-year-old daughter, Elizabeth, into bed with her at night.

In the early hours of the morning, they were woken by a mysterious scratching noise, sounding from behind the wainscoting, and Fanny convinced herself that it was the spirit of her dead sister warning her of her own imminent demise. When Kent returned he found his mistress on the verge of a nervous breakdown, and deemed it best that they move out. But no sooner had they found new lodgings than Fanny died of smallpox, and was buried in a vault in the church of St John's Clerkenwell.

When Kent began to press Parson's for repayment of the outstanding loan, the former reacted by claiming that the scratching noises had resumed in his house. Furthermore, he insisted that it was the spirit of Miss Fanny that was behind this latest outbreak, and that she had informed him that William Kent had, in fact, murdered her.

When news spread that a vengeful ghost was making its presence known at 33 Cock Lane, Londoners flocked to make its acquaintance, and heard the revenant of Miss Fanny – using a sequence of banging, scratching and knocking noises – accuse William Kent of poisoning her with arsenic. The activity appeared to centre on eleven-year-old Elizabeth Parsons, and her father was only too happy to decipher the messages. He also did a roaring trade, charging an admission fee to those who wanted to hear the ghost!

But then a local clergyman threw a holy spanner into the works by announcing that, since the spirit was apparently accusing Kent of a serious crime, then an investigation should be carried out by a group of eminent men into the veracity of the allegations. The ghost proved more than willing to oblige, and informed him, through Parsons, that if he would spend a night by Miss Fanny's final resting place in the crypt of St John's church then she would answer any

Haunted London

Cock Lane

questions by knocking on the lid of her coffin.

And so it was that the vicar, accompanied by a group of fearless companions that included the great Dr Samuel Johnson, traipsed down into St John's crypt at one o'clock one morning.

When nothing had occurred by dawn, Johnson declared the ghost a fraud. A secret watch was kept on Elizabeth, who was observed hiding a small wooden board under her stays, and the trick was exposed.

Parsons spent two years in the King's Bench Prison. Elizabeth was exonerated of any crime, it being deemed that she had been an unwitting accomplice. William Kent's name was cleared.

London settled back into the Age of Reason, and the ghost was assigned to the pages of history as Scratching Fanny of Cock Lane!

Continue along Giltspur Street, at the end of which go right along Holborn Viaduct, and immediately turn in through the church gates on the right to admire

11. THE CHURCH OF THE HOLY SEPULCHRE WITHOUT NEWGATE

Founded in 1137, and dedicated originally to St

Edmund, the fact that, like the Holy Sepulchre in Jerusalem, it stood just outside the north-west gate of the City made the church the favoured venue for the Knights of the Crusades to set out from on their journey to the Holy Land, and thus it acquired its present name.

It was rebuilt in 1450 and, although damaged by the Great Fire of London it wasn't destroyed, and thus the edifice that greets today's visitor is a veritable cornucopia of differing architectural styles.

During the Blitz of World War Two the nearby City Temple was destroyed, and its congregation were invited to make use of the church of St Sepulchre, as it was by then better known. As the vicar handed over the keys to the Temple's minister, Dr Weatherhead, he commented casually that, if he were alone in the church at night and happened to see a tall, pale clergyman, "Don't be alarmed; it's just a ghost." The vicar went on to explain, "He's quite often there, and when I speak to him he never answers."

A few Sundays later, following the morning service, Dr Weatherhead and his wife invited a female friend to dine with them. Over lunch, the woman, who had been told nothing of the haunting, informed the minister that on the occasions when she had watched him take communion at the church, she had noticed a "tall, pale-faced clergyman, with you in the Sanctuary. At first I thought he was assisting you and then one morning I saw you walk right through him, and I knew he was a ghost."

Exit the churchyard, turn left, go over Giltspur Street and, on the opposite corner, pause outside, or, better still, inside

12. THE VIADUCT TAVERN

The Viaduct Tavern stands opposite the Central Criminal Courts (better known the world over as the Old Bailey after the road in which they stand). It dates from 1875, and is the last example of a late Victorian gin palace left in the City of London.

It is also prone to suffer from bouts of poltergeist activity. 'Poltergeist' is derived from two German terms: *Poltern*, meaning 'to knock', and *Geist*, meaning 'spirit'. The restless spirit that haunts the Viaduct Tavern has a propensity to haunt the pub's cellars, where several members of staff have experienced its unwelcome attentions.

In 1982, the then landlord's daughter had been left in charge of the pub for a Sunday morning session. Having closed up, she went upstairs to the top room, where she sat on the sofa and began reading the newspaper. Suddenly, she heard footsteps come stomping up the stairs, the door flew open, her paper was snatched from her grip and then thrown to the floor. The door then slammed shut, and she heard the footsteps go back down the stairs. She searched the pub, but she could find no sign that anyone else was in there.

In 1987 a new manager took over the pub, and brought with him his faithful German Shepherd dog. Fearless as the dog was on most occasions, it would often sit looking at the cellar door, whimpering and whining, its hackled raised, staring at something that he could evidently see but which remained invisible to the patrons and landlord of the pub.

Throughout the 1990s the ghost got ever more mischievous, and would do things such as drink peoples' drinks when they weren't looking. It also had a fondness for flushing the ladies' toilet at the most inopportune of moments.

But, as often happens when there is a resident spook on one's premises, staff grew quite attached to their ghost and they gave him the name Fred. Whenever a customer would come up to the bar to complain that their drink had disappeared, or an irate lady returned from the toilet to complain that it had flushed when she wasn't expecting it to do so, they would be reassured that it was just Fred up to his tricks!

In 1996 a manager was tidying the cellar one Saturday morning, when the door suddenly slammed shut and the lights went out. Feeling his way to the door, he found that no matter how hard he pushed it just would not open. Fortunately, his wife heard his cries for help and came downstairs to investigate. She found that the doors, which would not open from the inside, were unlocked and easily pushed open from the outside.

In May 1999 two electricians, working in one of the pub's upstairs rooms, also attracted the ghost's unwelcome attentions. They had rolled up the carpet and were taking up the floorboards, when one of them felt a hand tap him on the shoulder. Thinking it was his workmate he turned round, but found that he was on the other side of the room. Believing he'd imagined it he went back to work, and yet again he felt a tap on his shoulder. Standing up, he went over to his friend to ask if he was playing a prank, but the man denied any involvement. As he was about to return to his chores, both men watched as the heavy carpet, that lay rolled up by the window, was lifted into the air and dropped heavily onto the floor.

On one occasion the pub was visited by a medium, who, having absorbed the unique ambience of the hostelry, walked up to the landlord before she left and informed him that the ghost was in fact "a Scottish gentleman called Robert, who would be much obliged if people would stop calling him Fred."

Before you leave the pub, be sure to ask the staff to allow you to visit the cellar, which is where much of the ghostly activity appears to emanate from. They will be only too happy to oblige, providing the pub is not too busy and you have bought a drink.

....

 Exit the pub, keep ahead along Newgate Street, and look over at

....

13. THE OLD BAILEY

The building dates from 1902, when it was built on the site of Newgate Prison. Its official name is The Central Court for England and Wales, albeit it is known the world over by the name of the street in which it stands: Old Bailey.

Numerous famous criminal trials have taken place

behind the walls that you are now looking over at. But one in particular is somewhat curious from a paranormal perspective.

When do you think the last witchcraft trial took place in England? Go on, have a guess. 17th century? 18th century? 19th century? Try again.

In fact, the last trial for witchcraft was held in England in March 1944 here at the Central Criminal Court, and the unfortunate witch who found herself on trial was the Scottish medium Victoria Helen McCrae Duncan (1897-1956).

In November 1941, during World War Two, Duncan held a séance in Portsmouth, in the course of which

the spirit of a sailor from HMS *Barham* materialised and revealed that his ship had been sunk. As it happened, the sinking of HMS *Barham* was, at the time, embargoed, and had not been made public other than to the relatives of the deceased sailors.

As a consequence of her revelation, the Navy began to take an interest into her activities and two lieutenants duly attended the séance she held on 14th January 1942. One of them, Lieutenant Worth, was not in the least bit impressed when a white figure materialised behind the curtain and claimed to be the spirit of his aunt. This was something of a surprise to Lieutenant Worth, since in fact he didn't actually have a deceased aunt. When a further figure appeared and claimed to be his sister, Worth responded by pointing out that his sister was, in fact, alive and well. Disgusted by what he saw as blatant fraud, Worth reported the seance to the police.

Five days later, an undercover policeman attended one of Mrs Duncan's séances, and watched as a white-shrouded apparition appeared in the room. This, as it transpired, was in fact Mrs Duncan herself, and having seized her the police officer arrested her.

Mrs Duncan was found in possession of a mocked-up HMS *Barham* hatband, which supposedly belonged to the spirit of a dead sailor on board the sunken ship, albeit since 1939 sailors' hatbands were emblazoned with 'HMS' and not the name of their ship.

Initially Mrs Duncan was charged under Section 4 of the 1824 Vagrancy Act, a minor offence that could be dealt with by magistrates. But the authorities considered the case to be so serious they looked for a more serious charge to bring against the unfortunate medium, and came upon Section 4 of the 1735 Witchcraft Act, which pertained specifically to fraudulent 'spiritual' activity, and was, therefore, trialable before a jury.

The case was a *cause célèbre* when it opened at the Old Bailey in March 1944. Many people took a great interest in the proceedings.

On Monday, 27th March 1944, her defending counsel even offered to hold a séance in court in order that Mrs Duncan's spirit guide might aid her defence.

"It is the acid test," he told the hushed court. "If Mrs Duncan has a guide, he will be with her now, probably trying to help her here in the Central Criminal Court."

The Judge, Sir Gerald Dodson, replied that there was no use wasting the time of the jury with some sort of demonstration.

Despite the fact that the police, on raiding the séance in Portsmouth, had actually found no evidence of the usual fraudulent props such as cheesecloth to facilitate the spirit manifestation, Mrs Duncan was found Guilty, and was sent to prison for nine months.

Winston Churchill was so disgusted by the case that he fired off an angry missive to the Home Secretary, Herbert Morrison, demanding to know why a piece of "obsolete tomfoolery" was being used in "a modern court of justice."

As a direct result of the trial, the Witchcraft Act was repealed in 1951, and was replaced by the Fraudulent Mediums Act.

Continue along Newgate Street, noting on the left a little way along the blue plaque on the wall marking the former site of the Greyfriars Monastery. A little further along, turn left, then right into the churchyard of

14. CHRISTCHURCH GREYFRIARS

This is the site of an ancient burial ground where lie the mortal remains of 'the she-wolf of France', Queen Isabella, wife of the English King Edward II. With her lover, Roger Mortimer, she instigated the deposing of the King and had him imprisoned at Berkeley Castle.

On the night of 21st September, 1327, he was brutally

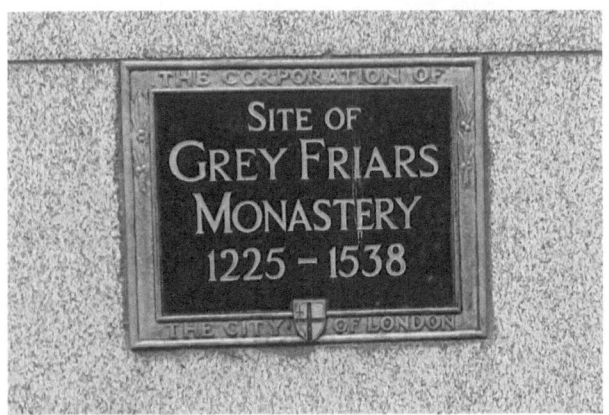

murdered by way of 'a kind of horn or funnel... thrust into his fundament through which a red-hot spit was run up his bowels'.

His screams could be heard far outside the castle walls, and are still heard there on the anniversary of the horrific event.

Following Mortimer's execution by the King's son, Edward III, in 1330, Isabella retreated into a polite retirement. She died in 1358, her last years having been racked by violent dementia.

She was buried here at Greyfriars, with the heart of Edward II placed upon her breast. At twilight, her beautiful, angry ghost flits amongst the trees and bushes, clutching the beating heart of her murdered husband before her.

Agnes Cotell was considered a great beauty of the Tudor age. Her first husband was John Cotell, steward to Sir Edward Hungerford, the owner of Farleigh Hungerford Castle, in Somerset. On 26th July, 1518, John died, supposedly having been strangled by two assassins hired by Agnes. John's body was, so tradition holds, then burned in the kitchen oven at Farleigh Hungerford Castle.

Agnes didn't stay single long, for she had soon attracted the eye of Sir Edward himself, and the couple were married, with the result she now became Lady Alice Hungerford.

But, when her second husband died, on 24th January 1522, questions were asked and it wasn't long before she found herself arrested on charges of having murdered her first husband. Found guilty, she was hanged at Tyburn on 20th February 1522 and was, so tradition holds, buried within the precincts of the Greyfriars Monastery, where her beautiful, serene phantom was soon seen drifting through the cloisters and aisles of the monastery and subsequently, following its dissolution, through the burial ground that sprang up on its site.

And so the two ladies went about their nocturnal

rambles, each blissfully unaware of the other's existence, until one night, in Victorian times, they met among the tombs. Eyeing each other with surprise, then curiosity and finally hostility, they each became jealous of the other's beauty, and a fearsome battle erupted as they fought over their territory.

Bemused witnesses could only look on in terror as the spectral fight became more and more vicious. A night watchman, caught up in the midst of the ghostly squabbling, was so frightened by the experience that he fled the scene and "never... came back to collect his pay."

Backtrack along Newgate Street, and on arrival at the traffic lights cross them, and make your way left onto Warwick Lane. Keep ahead and, on arrival at Amen Corner, go right and pause outside the gates of

15. AMEN COURT

Amen Court comprises a delightful enclave of 18th and 19th century houses, where the Dean and Chapter of St Paul's Cathedral live. Famous past residents have included wit and author Sidney Smith, who lived at number 1 from 1831-1834, and R.H. Barnham, author of the evocative and eerie *Ingoldsby Legends*, who occupied the same address from 1839-1845.

At the rear of the court, behind the bushes, there looms a large and ominous dark wall, behind which once stood the fearsome bulk of Newgate Prison, until its demolition in 1902. However, on the other side of the wall, there still is a tiny passage, which was known as 'Deadman's Walk' in the days of the prison, on account of the fact that prisoners were led along it to their executions, and were buried beneath it afterwards.

Although many ghostly tales have evolved around this sinister old wall, the most chilling is that of the Black Dog of Newgate. This shapeless black form slithers along the top of the wall, slides sloppily down into the courtyard, and then melts away. Its manifestations are always accompanied by a nauseous smell, and are often accompanied by the sound of dragging footsteps.

Its origins are said to date back to the reign of Henry III, when a fearsome famine struck London, and the poor felons incarcerated within Newgate Prison, faced with the prospect of starvation, turned to cannibalism as a means of survival.

One day a scholar was imprisoned there on charges of sorcery. His portly figure proved too much of a temptation for the older inmates, and within a few days they killed and ate him, pronouncing him to be "good meate."

However, they soon had cause to regret their actions, for a hideous black dog with eyes of fire and jowls that dripped with blood appeared in the dead of night and proceeded to exact a terrifying revenge. Some hapless prisoners were torn limb from limb by the ferocious beast, as their anguished screams echoed through the gaol, striking terror into the very souls of the other inmates. Others simply died of fright, when they heard its ghostly panting and its heavy paws padding towards them across the cold, stone floors.

Those who survived the first nights of its lust for blood and vengeance became so terrified that they killed their guards and escaped. But, no matter how far they travelled, the beast hunted them down one by one. Only when the murder of its master, the Sorcerer, had been fully avenged did it return to the prison's fetid dungeons, where it became a hideous harbinger of death, always appearing on the eve of executions or the night before a felon breathed his last.

When the prison was demolished in 1902 it was hoped that the Black Dog would become a thing of the past. But it was not to be.

For people walking in Amen Court at night, who have happened to glance at the dark wall, have

Edgar's Guide To...

Haunted London

Deadman's Walk, Newgate

reported seeing its seething black shape, shuffling across the wall, and have watched as it slithers into the courtyard where it disappears before their very eyes, leaving the smell of death its ghostly wake.

Another ghost associated with the courtyard is that of Amelia Dyer, the 'Reading Baby Farmer.' Paid to look after unwanted babies, this evil woman would drown her charges in the Thames and other rivers, whilst continuing to draw a substantial income for their upkeep.

Brought to justice, she was sentenced to death and, on 10th June 1896, she took her final stroll along Deadman's Walk. As she did so, she passed a young warder named Mr Scott. Stopping abruptly, she slowly turned towards him and fixed him with her evil gaze. Her small, dark eyes looked into his, her face cracked into a toothless smile and, in a low, rasping voice, she sneered, "I'll meet you again some day, sir." Moments later, she was dead, dangling at the end of the hangman's noose.

The years passed. Scott progressed in his chosen career, and memories of Amelia Dyer and her prophecy were soon forgotten. Then one night, just before the prison was to close, he found himself along in the warders' room, his back to the grille that looked out onto Deadman's Walk. Suddenly, a cold shiver ran

Amelia Dyer's Chamber of Horrors waxwork

down his spine and got the distinct impression that someone was watching him. And then he heard it, that low, sneering, rasp as the unmistakable voice of Mrs Dyer echoed from the passage: "Meet you again, meet you again..."

Turning, he saw her evil face, framed by the grille, grinning at him. Stirred to action he rushed at her, but she promptly vanished. Throwing open the door, the passage was silent and empty.

Had he imagined it? Possibly, yet he could never account for the woman's handkerchief which, at that very moment, fluttered to the flagstones and lay still by his feet.

Backtrack, go right along Ave Maria Lane (as Warwick Lane has now become), cross to its left side and go left along Ludgate Hill to pause outside

16. ST PAUL'S CATHEDRAL

Just inside the left door as you face the Cathedral, you will find the Kitchener Chapel. Its walls are adorned with an assortment of battle colours, and on its floor reclines a white marble effigy of General Kitchener (1850-1916), Secretary of War from 1914, whose death, on 3rd June 1916, was treated as a

national calamity.

If, as you stand gazing upon his memorial, a sudden chill passes over you, take note, for this is often the first hint that the Cathedral's ghostly resident, 'Whistler', is about to put in an appearance. Next, you will hear the low, barely audible sound of mournful whistling. Gazing into the chapel you may spy an old, wizened clergyman who has flowing locks of grey hair and is dressed in old-fashioned robes. His doleful, though tuneless whistling will grow steadily louder as he glides across the chapel and melts slowly away into the wall to the right of the gates. Everyone who has seen him has attested to the fact that he always follows the same time-worn path, and that he always vanishes into the same section of the wall.

Intriguingly, during the renovation work following the 1914-18 War, when it was decided that the chapel (then known as the All Souls Chapel) should be re-dedicated to General Kitchener, workmen uncovered a hidden door secreted behind the exact section of wall where the ghost always disappears. It opened onto a narrow, winding staircase that led up to a secret room within the inner fabric of the main body of the cathedral. Nobody had known of its existence, or purpose, with, of course, the exception of the ghost, whoever he may have been in his lifetime.

Cross Ludgate Hill via the traffic lights, veer left on their other side, and go first right into Dean's Court, where, a little way along on the right is

17. THE OLD DEANERY

The Old Deanery was built in 1670 by Sir Christopher Wren, and was formerly the residence of the Dean of St Paul's Cathedral. Local tradition holds this to be a haunted building, a claim vociferously disputed by Martin Sullivan, Dean of St Paul's until his retirement in 1977.

The strange creaks that were often heard by members of his family and staff he put down to the antiquity of the building. The bumps and clanks that were often heard at night he dismissed as "nothing more than the central heating getting on a bit."

He did, however, confess to being slightly bemused by a toilet-roll holder that would go 'decidedly wonky' whenever anyone else looked at it, but which had always righted itself by the time the Dean was called to repair it. But then he added: "Since I can't conceive of a haunted toilet-roll holder, I can only put it down to my skill at do-it-yourself."

Continue to the end of Dean's Court and go right along Carter Lane. This was once one of the City's main thoroughfares. The large colourful building on your right is the City of London Youth Hostel, originally the St Paul's Choir School – hence the bright ecclesiastical motifs and Latin inscriptions that adorn the facade. Take the second turning left, which will take you through a covered passage and into

---

18. WARDROBE PLACE

This glimpse of bygone London dates from 1720. To stand here on a winter's night, when the lights of the neighbouring buildings have been switched off, is to experience the true thrill of historic and haunted London.

Massive plane trees tower over the three-storey houses, and even the faintest of breezes will set their branches creaking and their trunks swaying. The stillness of the yard keeps you constantly on edge, passing darting glances around the gloomy shadows, feeling certain that unseen eyes are watching you from the inky blackness of the house windows.

Not surprisingly, the courtyard has a ghost. People going about their honest, night-time toil in the neighbourhood have reported sighting a lady, dressed all in white, drifting aimlessly from door to door.

Who she is and why she should choose to wander this courtyard is unknown. She says nothing, does nothing, and pays little heed to anyone or anything, being more than content to let the world pass her by as she goes about her ghostly business. But, should someone be so rude as to stare at her, she takes umbrage and responds by fading into nothingness.

Backtrack to Carter Lane and turn left. Go first left and descend St Andrew's Hill. Veer left past the Cockpit Tavern, and then, immediately to the left of the

Shaw Booksellers Pub & Eating House, go up the steps to stand before the Church of

....

19. ST ANDREW-BY-THE-WARDROBE

The unusual name of this red-brick church, which was built by Sir Christopher Wren in 1695, refers to its former proximity to the King's Wardrobe, a suite of neighbouring buildings where robes of state and cloth for the royal household were stored, until its destruction during the Great Fire of London, after which the wardrobe was moved to Westminster.

St Andrew-by-the-Wardrobe

In 1933, three bells from the parish church at Avenbury, in Herefordshire, were re-hung in the belfry of St Andrew's-by-the-Wardrobe. One of them, known as Gabriel, had been cast in Worcester in the 15th century, and it was an established piece of Avenbury folklore that, whenever a vicar of the church died, then this particular bell would always ring out of its own accord to mourn his passing.

Barely a year after its arrival here in the City of London, local residents were woken in the early hours of one morning by the knell of a solitary bell, sounding from the tower of St Andrew's church. When local police arrived to investigate they found the church was locked, and a cursory search revealed no sign of a forced entry. The night was still, with not even the faintest breeze blowing, and yet many people had heard the bell tolling, though none could explain how, or why, it could have happened. But then next morning word arrived that, shortly before the mysterious chime had been heard, the vicar at Avenbury had died.

....

Pass to the right of the church tower, turn left, then descend the steep flight of steps on the right, to turn right along Queen Victoria Street. Keep ahead until you arrive at the wonderful Blackfriars Pub, where the Haunted City walk ends.

 If you wish to continue your ghostly trek by moving on to the Haunted West End walk, take a tube from Blackfriars Underground Station opposite to Embankment, which is just two stops along the Circle and District Lines.

PART TWO: THE HAUNTED WEST END

Map on inner back cover

Start: Embankment Underground Station, Villiers Street exit

End: Berkeley Square, W1J 6AB

Duration: 2½ to 3 hours

Best of Times: Evenings

Oh, what a wickedly spooky walk this one is. From the gardens that line the River Thames you will descend into a chilling vault, where echoes of a long-ago act of infamy are still sometimes heard in the chilling shadows.

Then there is the top people's bank, which was once so afflicted by a ghost in its computer room that they called in a medium to rid them of the troublesome wraith. And then we duck into a chilling alleyway to make our way to the scene of one of the late 19th-century's most notorious murders, that robbed the stage of one of its greatest and most popular actors but gave the seeker of the supernatural another spectral form to look for.

Want to find a haunted theatre? We've got several for you. Curious about how many haunted pubs there are in the West End of London? We've got a goodly smattering of those for you to enjoy as well.

And that's without the haunted park in which you will try to decide which tree is the notorious 'Tree of Death', or the two royal palaces where notorious acts from the mists of time are still repeated on their anniversaries.

And, if all this isn't sufficient to get you out and about on the streets of the haunted West End, then how about the tour's grand finale, the most haunted house in London?

Chills and thrills await you!

HIGHLIGHTS OF THE HAUNTED WEST END WALK

Here are some of the highlights you will shiver at as you make your way through London's haunted West End street:

- The sinister arch, where a long-ago murder is played out over and over again, much to the terror of those who witness it.

- The stage door of a theatre where a popular Victorian actor was murdered, and to which he returns time and time again.

- The theatre where a former manageress often turns up to enjoy the first night of performances, despite the fact she's been dead for almost 1000 years.

- The Royal place where a brutal event that happened many hundreds of years ago is said to be repeated each year on the anniversary of the act of infamy.

- The Tree of Death, around which many a story of terror and mayhem is woven.

- The house that once had a reputation that was so sinister, history simply remembers it as the Most Haunted House in London. And you'll stand outside it... but for how long?

Edgar's Guide To...

To begin, leave Embankment Underground Station via the Villiers Street Exit and ascend Villiers Street, keeping to its right side by the park railings. As the park ends, turn right down the steps of Watergate Walk, passing on your left, the steps that lead into the wonderfully atmospheric Gordon's Wine Bar. If time permits it is well worth making a refreshment stop here, as there is no venue quite like it anywhere else in London. It is cavernous, candlelit place, stepped in history and brimming with ambience. A little way along Watergate Walk, on your right, you come to

1. THE YORK WATERGATE

An elaborate and exquisitely-carved stone structure that found itself marooned on dry land when, in the 1860s, Sir Joseph Bazalgette embanked the Thames and pushed its shoreline a considerable distance southwards. The gate was built in 1626 by George Villiers, first Duke of Buckingham, and was intended as the river entrance to his grand London home, York House. The rings that the boats could be moored up at can still be glimpsed through the gates of the structure.

Haunted London

The York Watergate

☞ *Having admired the gate to your heart's content, make your way up the stairs opposite it, and keep ahead along Buckingham Street, and pause outside number 12 on the left, which was built in 1677, and where a plaque on the wall remembers the diarist Samuel Pepys (1633-1703).*

2. PEPYS'S GENIAL PHANTOM

By the time he came to live here, in 1679, Pepys had spent several months in the Tower of London, to which he had been sent in the May of that year, on charges of "Piracy, Popery and Treachery."

Following his release in July 1679, he took refuge here with his friend and former employee Will Hewer, who afforded Pepys, "all the care, kindness and faithfulness of a son."

It would appear that Pepys felt a great affinity to the house in his lifetime; so much so, that his ghost has been known to return to it in death, "a greyish figure with a genial smiling face" that strolls briskly down the stairs inside, and which has also been known to look down from the upper windows on passers-by below.

....

Continue along Buckingham Street, turn right along John Adam Street, go next right along York Buildings, and take the next left into Lower Robert Street to descend into the encroaching gloom of one of the few surviving

....

Samuel Pepys

3. ADELPHI ARCHES

The area was developed between 1768 and 1774 by the brothers Robert James and William Adam, on land that sloped steeply down to the River Thames. The developers overcame the problems by building a vast network of arches to support the streets above which, by the 19th century, had attracted a vast homeless community, seeking the meagre shelter afforded by them, and their reputation was such that they were considered something of a curiosity.

Dickens, writing in *David Copperfield*, referred to them when he recalled how his most autobiographical character was fond of "wandering about the Adelphi because it was a mysterious place with those dark arches."

The following article, which appeared in the *Cornish Times* on Saturday, 28th November 1857, provides us with a glimpse of what might have awaited you had you undertaken the descent you are about to make in the mid-19th century:

"Few portions of that huge labyrinth, the great metropolis, have been so little visited by strangers as the Adelphi Arches, better known the 'Dark Arches', though we know not of their parallel anywhere.

A passing wayfarer down the Strand may have noticed certain dark archways on the south side; he may have

Adelphi Arch

noticed, too, if topographically observant, that the Adelphi buildings stand on level ground, whereas the streets on either hand slope abruptly towards the river.

Those yawning mouths lead to long avenues, ramifications of damp vaulted passages, which constitute altogether the Adelphi Arches. The next time he is in the neighbourhood, let him enter, and explore the labyrinth to its furthest recesses; let him, indeed, do this twice; in the day time, and again at night; for night alone can reveal the scenes of existence which that labyrinth discloses.

Reader – think what our condition would be without a home, without a supper, and without a bed. Some thirty thousand such there are every night all the year through in this great hive of bricks and mortar, to whom an archway, some place whither they may escape from the elements, and from the noisy turmoil of life without, stands in place of home. The railway arches come in for their share, and the dry arches of bridges, but all sink into insignificance in comparison with the labyrinth of vaulted passages which we are about ideally to explore.

The entrance is steep and slippery, always damp when the weather is dry. Vainly the neighbouring sewers yawn and gape up through their grating prison bars to catch whatever of slush and impurity may chance to pass their way. The Adelphi Arches have insatiate maw for filth. Down the flowing pollutions come, and in they roll. As you cautiously tread your way, each passing footfall reverberates like the clanking of fetters. If you speak, your words come back again, like voices of whispering ghouls, with which, indeed, it takes no great stretch of the imagination to picture the labyrinth as peopled."

JENNY'S GHOST

Inevitably, some of the women who sought shelter here resorted to prostitution as a means of raising a few pennies with which to purchase a few comforts to alleviate the harshness of their everyday existences.

One such inhabitant was a girl whom tradition simply remembers as 'Poor Jenny', who was reputedly murdered by a client she had taken to the grim bundle of filthy rags that passed for her bed.

The screams of her final moments are said to echo through the chilling subterranean world of shadows in which you now find yourself, and the rhythmic tapping of her feet drumming on the cold stones in her final death throes have also been said to echo through the vaults around you.

Adelphi Arch

☞ *Linger as long as you dare, and then backtrack to the reassuring safety of York Buildings, turn right and cross over John Adam Street, and keep ahead through George Court. Go up the stairs at the far end, and cross West Strand via the pedestrian crossing, turning left on the other side. A little way along, pause outside*

4. COUTTS BANK

This is London's largest private bank, and, at first glance, not the type of building you would expect to be haunted, but hang on in there my fearless spectre-seekers, for, in November 1993, it was reported in the newspapers that a restless wraith was wreaking night-time havoc in the bank's computer room. He had even given a receptionist a nasty shock when he materialised before her, minus his head.

A ghost in the computer room was one thing, but a headless phantom startling employees at the top person's bank was another matter altogether, and the directors sought the assistance of the medium Eddie Burks to see if his talents could solve the mystery of why this visitor from the spirit world had begun causing trouble here.

Burks had soon made contact with the ghost, and was able to name him as Thomas Howard, 4th Duke of Norfolk, who had been beheaded in 1572, having plotted to marry Mary, Queen of Scots and depose Elizabeth I in favour of his new spouse.

It isn't recorded as to whether Howard was *sans* head during his conversation with Burks – although one presumes he couldn't have been, as he was able to bemoan the fact that, "I was beheaded on a summer's day. I have held much bitterness and... I must let this go. In the name of God I ask your help. I cannot do this alone."

Burks got to work, and was able to persuade the ghostly nobleman to move on and trouble the good folk of Coutts no longer.

On 15th November, 1993, a service attended by the then Duke and Duchess of Norfolk was held to pray for the repose of the soul of their ancestor at a nearby church. On leaving, the modern Duke was asked by a reporter if he was pleased by the fact that his ancestor was now at rest. "Actually," replied the Duke, "I don't believe in ghosts."

....

 Backtrack along West Strand, keep ahead past Agar Street onto Strand, go over Bedford Street,

and, having passed the Adelphi Theatre, go left into the deliciously spooky Bull Inn Court, and pause outside or, if the urge takes you, pop into the tiny

5. NELL GWYNNE TAVERN

To the left of the door as you enter, staff and customers alike have spoken, in whispered tones, of a strange coldness that has been known to hang heavy in the air. Gentlemen have been known to feel a spectral hand tapping them on the back pocket, but, on turning, have found nobody there.

A visiting medium once told the landlord that she could sense the spirit of an old man who had apparently been a former tenant at the pub. He was, so the medium stated, extremely pleased with the way that the pub was being run, but should he ever be dissatisfied, he would make his displeasure known to those he held responsible for interfering with the efficient running of what he still saw as his pub.

Continue to the far end of Bull Inn Court, turn left along Maiden Lane and pause on the left outside the back of the Adelphi Theatre, where a green plaque on the wall remembers

The entrance to Bull Inn Court and the Nell Gwynne Tavern

Edgar's Guide To...

William Terriss

6. THE MURDER OF WILLIAM TERRISS

William Terriss was the matinee idol of the late Victorian era. With his charisma, good looks and suaveness of manner he was, quite simply, a STAR. He was a hugely popular actor – and, I think I can safely say, he was nothing less than the Johnny Depp, Tom Cruise, Daniel Craig or Brad Pitt of his day – and the crowds flocked to watch him perform in the melodramas for which the Strand's Adelphi Theatre was renowned.

At the time of his death Terriss was wowing audiences in his role as Captain Thorne in the play *Secret Service*.

He spent the afternoon of Thursday, 16th December 1897 playing whist at his West End club. At around 4.00pm he returned to his residence and spent some time in the company of one of his oldest friends, Mr Henry Graves.

Just before 7.00pm that evening they took a cab to the Adelphi Theatre and, having been dropped off at the junction of Bedford Street and Maiden Lane, they proceeded to walk along Maiden Lane to the private stage door of the Adelphi Theatre that was only used by Terriss and two of the other principals of the company. This door adjoined the Royal Stage Door, which can still be seen to your right, and which still has the royal crest emblazoned above it.

As they approached the door, Terriss said to Graves, "Wait a minute Harry till I get my keys," whereupon he proceeded to take his keys from his pocket and then, stooping slightly, put his key in the door.

As he did so, according to Graves's later testimony, "...somebody rushed from across the road and struck him two blows most rapidly on the back..." So quickly did events unfold that Graves, and indeed several passers-by, later said that they at first mistook the action as being nothing more sinister than a friendly pat on the back, although he did comment that it had occurred to him "how exceedingly rough the act of friendship was." Terriss himself appears to have thought likewise and he turned to face his attacker, whereupon his assailant raised his arm a third time and plunged a large knife deep into the actor's chest.

At this point Terriss, realising the seriousness of the situation, cried out, "My God, I am stabbed; arrest him," whereupon several of the theatre scene-shifters came to his aid and, according to one newspaper report, "formed all too late a bodyguard." They carried him into the stage door passage and propped him up on pillows, and placed ice upon his chest.

Doctors Walter H. Morgan and W. Curling Hayward, of the nearby Charing Cross hospital, were quickly summoned to the scene and they arrived at 7.30pm. They found the stricken actor lying in the stage door

The Adelphi Theatre in 1896, the year before Terriss's murder

passage, where the stage hands had placed him.

On examining the patient, the doctors discovered the three stab wounds, one of which – situated on the left of the chest, directly above the heart – according to newspaper reports "would have been sufficient to cause death." The doctors instructed that he be carried to a sofa in his dressing room where, so witnesses reported, he made one or two faint attempts to speak, although he did not appear to be conscious.

As it transpired he was beyond medical help and, according to Dr. Hayward's later testimony, "he was sinking very fast – his death took place at two or three minutes to eight – during that time he was semi-conscious."

Unaware of the drama unfolding backstage, the audience were, at that very moment, filing into the theatre to take their seats for that night's performance. Such was Terriss's popularity that the house was full, and the management was left with the unenviable task of informing the eager audience that the performance was to be cancelled that night. One can only imagine the nervousness with which the theatre's official faced the house, almost all of whom had no knowledge of the tragedy that had occurred, to inform them that "Mr Terriss had met with such a serious accident that he would be totally unable to appear that night."

The audience were given the option of a full refund or the opportunity to exchange their tickets for another night. As he left the stage cries of "understudy" sounded out. But, gradually, these diminished and the disappointed audience began filing out into the Strand.

In the street outside the theatre Henry Graves had kept a close eye on the assassin and, amidst the general pandemonium and cries of "murder" and "police", he, according to his later testimony, "followed the man and never lost sight of him for a moment." Giving evidence later in court, he stated:

"...a constable came up and I said 'I charge this man with stabbing Mr. Terriss' – I cannot say exactly how far he had got from the door of the theatre when the constable came up, it was some little distance – I and the constable went with the prisoner to the police-station; the prisoner walked very quietly, he was in the middle and the constable and I were on either side of him – he said nothing when I gave him in charge – on the way to the station I said to the prisoner 'What could have induced you to do such a cruel deed?' – he said 'Mr. Terriss would not allow me to have any employment, and I did it,' either 'in revenge,' or 'by way of revenge,' I am not quite certain which – when the prisoner was charged at the station I returned to the theatre, and found Mr. Terriss lying at the foot of the stairs, he was dying then, and he died in my presence shortly afterwards..."

The constable in question was PC John Bragg, who later stated how,

"On December 16th, about 7.30 in the evening, I heard cries of murder and police in Maiden Lane – I went there and found Mr. Graves and the prisoner about 100 yards from the private door of the theatre, towards Southampton street – Mr. Graves said, 'I give this man into custody for stabbing Mr. Terriss.' – I took

hold of the prisoner – he said, 'What is the matter?' – I said, 'You know what is the matter.' – On the way to the station, Mr. Graves said, 'What made you do such a dreadful, bloody thing as that?' – He said, 'In revenge, he blackmailed me for 10 years.' – He used the word 'black-mailing', two or three times – On the road to the station he also said, 'I have given him due warning plenty of times.' – He also said, 'I should either have to die in the street, or have my revenge.' – Inspector Wood took the charge at the station."

Inspector George Wood was on duty at Bow Street Police Station when the door opened and the accused was brought in. The first to speak was Henry Graves, who announced, "This man has stabbed Mr. William Terriss at Maiden Lane, as he was about to enter the stage door of the Adelphi Theatre."

The inspector asked where the weapon was, at which the prisoner threw back the Inverness cape he was wearing and produced a large, bloodstained knife from his coat pocket. Handing it to the inspector he informed him, with no hint of remorse, "That is what I stabbed him with; he had due warning, and if he is dead he knows what he had to expect from me. He prevented me from getting assistance from the Actor's Benevolent Fund to-day, and I have stopped him."

The accused then gave his name as Richard Archer

from The Illustrated Police News, 25th December 1897

Prince, of 16 Eaton Court, Eaton Lane, Buckingham Palace Road. It later transpired that the accused was not only known to William Terriss, but he was in fact a fellow actor who had appeared in several plays alongside him. However, it was more than evident that Prince was mentally unstable and, as a consequence of his bad-tempered outbursts and erratic behaviour, he had found himself without roles and, as a result, facing extreme financial hardship. This exacerbated his mental instability and, by late 1897, he was a ticking time-bomb.

Evidently, he had come to blame Terriss for his predicament, despite the fact that Terriss had shown him considerable kindness, and had even recommended him for assistance from the Actor's Benevolent Fund, based in Adam Street, just off the Strand. But funds from even this source had not been recently forthcoming, and his paranoia regarding William Terriss was growing.

The crime, it seems, had been premeditated, and there were several warning signs that Terriss had been in danger. Henry Spratt, the stage doorkeeper at the Adelphi Theatre, for example, testified that, at the end of October or the beginning of November Prince had come to the stage-door and asked him to convey a letter to Mr. Terriss, and get an answer. Spratt recalled:

"I got an answer after about half-an-hour – I conveyed that answer to the prisoner – I said, 'The answer to the letter is All right.' After that I noticed him about the stage-door on several occasions – he was round the stage-door about six times altogether – he was there for about half an hour – Mr. Terriss was not in the habit of using the stage-door himself – he went in at a private door in Maiden Lane, of which he had a key – I remember on Wednesday, December 15th, the prisoner coming and speaking to me – it was about 6.50, or it might have been later. He said, 'Mr. Terriss comes up this way, doesn't he?' meaning the stage-door – I said, 'Yes' – that was the last I saw of him.

At Prince's Old Bailey trial, witnesses and doctors alike testified to his unstable state of mind. Henry Charles Bastian, Physician to the Hospital For Paralysis and Epilepsy, visited Prince in Holloway Prison and told the trial that:

"I connect the act of killing Mr. Terriss with the delusions – I think the act he did was to a certain extent the outcome of the delusions themselves; he believed he was persecuted by Mr. Terriss for eight or ten years, and undoubtedly there was a connection between the act and the delusions – I do not think he was capable of exercising self-control at the time; taking the state of his mind as it had existed for some years, and then taking the privations and troubles he had had, I have no doubt

he had no proper control."

Under cross examination Dr Bastian went into detail about Prince's lack of remorse regarding the murder:

"...He spoke with what I may call a most off-hand manner, and an air of levity about the act; there was no sign whatever of remorse for the act he had committed; indeed, he seemed to think it was an act of justice that Mr. Terriss should have been killed, and, as far as I could make out, that act of justice was brought about in some way through an intervention of the Almighty, and I think that notion I gathered then is really borne out by his demeanour and actions in Court to-day; he does not seem to be overladen with any feeling of remorse..."

In giving their verdict, the jury found Prince Guilty of the murder, adding that they found the prisoner knew what he was doing and to whom he was doing it; but that upon the medical evidence, he was insane so as not to be responsible for his actions according to law at the time he committed the act.

He was duly sentenced to be "detained until Her Majesty's pleasure be known," and was sent to Broadmoor Criminal Lunatic Asylum, where he became involved in entertainment for the inmates and conducted the prison orchestra until his death in 1936.

THE GHOST OF WILLIAM TERRISS

In 1928, a tourist walking along Maiden Lane was surprised to encounter a figure dressed in what he described as "old-fashioned turn-of-the-century clothing." He was about to make a comment about the man's outdated fashion sense, when, to his utter astonishment, the figure vanished into thin air, "like a bubble bursting." Later, when shown a picture of Terriss, he was adamant that he was the man whom he had seen.

An actress, resting in her dressing room one afternoon, was suddenly gripped by the arms, and the chaise lounge on which she was reclining began to rock violently from side to side. A green light then appeared above the mirror, and two loud knocks were heard sounding out. Everything then went quiet.

She later learnt that her dressing room was once the dressing room of Jessica Milward, Terriss's leading lady, and that he was in the habit of knocking twice on the door whenever he past it.

Continue along Maiden Lane, cross over Bedford Street, and keep ahead along Chandos Place. Notice the plaque up on the wall of TGI Friday's marking the fact that Charles Dickens worked here as a boy (not at TGI Friday's, incidentally, but at Warren's Blacking premises that stood on this site. Keep ahead over Agar Street, walk past Charing Cross Police Station, and veer diagonally right across the road towards Bedfordbury, and make your way through the narrow, gloomy and wonderfully sinister Brydges Place, On arrival at the far end, turn right into St Martin's Lane, and pause outside

....

7. THE LONDON COLISEUM

The theatre was designed by Frank Matcham for the impresario Oswald Stoll. It was intended as the largest and finest music hall of the age, a "people's palace of entertainment." With an audience capacity of 2,359 seats, this is the largest theatre in London.

For a short time during World War One the theatre was haunted by the ghost of a soldier, who had attended a show here on his last night of leave. Returning to the front, he was killed on 3rd October, 1918, and that very night his ghost was seen strolling down the gangway as the house lights dimmed. He turned into the second row of the dress circle and promptly disappeared. He made several repeat appearances, and then faded into theatrical history.

Continue along St Martin's Lane, crossing to its left side and pause outside

8. THE DUKE OF YORK'S THEATRE

The theatre was built in 1892 by Frank Wyatt and his wife, the actress and theatre manager Violet Melnotte. She owned the theatre for the next forty years, and was an eccentric and formidable presence.

Following Wyatt's death in 1926, Violet found herself embroiled in scandal when, in 1934, at the age of seventy-nine, she announced plans to marry the theatre's general manager, 31-year-old Archibald Patrick Moore. Such was the public outcry that the marriage plans were shelved and, since her children had pre-deceased her, Violet considered adopting him in order that he could inherit the theatre, although this plan too was shelved.

Violet Melnotte was renowned for refusing to reveal her actual age, and for never missing a first night at the theatre. Following her death on Tuesday, 17th September 1935, one newspaper remembered her fondly as "A white-haired old woman, gaily-dressed and powdered, she would sit in state wearing jewels and orchids."

However, her ghost likes to keep up her first night attendance record, and she is often seen mingling with modern audiences on first nights.

The theatre has another haunting that occurred in the late 1940s, and which has become legendary in both theatrical and paranormal circles.

Among the costumes worn in the production *The Queen Came By* was an old bolero-style jacket that acquired a sinister reputation for attempting to strangle any actress who wore it. No matter how much it was let out, actresses would complain that it would, apparently, start to shrink the moment they put it on, and of how it would grow tighter and tighter around them.

In an attempt to solve the mystery of what lay behind the phenomenon, a séance was held and one of the mediums present clearly saw a man attempting to drown a struggling young woman. Eventually her body collapsed, limp and lifeless, and the man proceeded remove her clothing, including her bolero-style jacket. He then wrapped her corpse in a blanket and carried it away.

With such an apparently sinister heritage, the jacket was considered an unsuitable prop and it was sold on to an American collector of Victoriana. When his wife tried the jacket on, she too experienced

Violet Melnotte in 1918

the uncomfortable sensation of strangulation. The garment's whereabouts have, thankfully, long since become unknown!

☞ *Continue along St Martin's Lane, passing Cecil Court on your left, which was reputedly the inspiration for Diagon Alley in the Harry Potter stories. Keep going, passing the Salisbury pub, a fine old Victorian establishment with snug bars, shadowy corners, and an atmosphere that makes it well worth a visit – albeit the only spirits to be found within are those behind the bar! Just past the pub, pause outside*

9. THE NOEL COWARD THEATRE

This theatre was built for Sir Charles Wyndham (1837-1919), although its original name was The New Theatre. In 1973 the name was changed to The Albery, in memory of Sir Bronson Albery (1881-1971), who managed it for many years.

In 1920 Noel Coward (1899-1973) made his West End debut here in the role of Bobbie Dermott in his own play, *I'll Leave It To You*. In 1973 Delfont Mackintosh purchased the building, and renamed it The Noel Coward Theatre.

The ghost that haunts this lovely theatre is that of its founder, Sir Charles Wyndham. On one occasion the actor Barry Jones was chatting with a fellow cast member, having taken a break from rehearsing, when

Sir Charles Wyndham

an elegantly-attired man with wavy grey hair came strolling towards them. They moved aside to allow him to pass, and, as he did so, the man nodded his appreciation, headed onto the stage and turned out of sight.

The man's old-fashioned attire intrigued Barry Jones, so he went and asked the door attendant who the man was. The attendant was adamant that nobody had passed him, and he was certain that there was nobody in the building who resembled the description that Jones gave of the man.

Some time later, Jones happened on a portrait of the theatre's founder, Sir Charles Wyndham, and immediately recognised him as the man whose appearance had so intrigued him.

Make your way through St Martin's Court, and at its other end turn left along Charing Cross Road. Keep straight until you arrive, on the left, outside

10. THE GARRICK THEATRE

Not many theatres are so impressed by their ghost that they decide to put a plaque on the exterior giving details of their resident spectre, but the Garrick

Theatre does just that!

The theatre was built in 1899 for W.S. Gilbert, of Gilbert and Sullivan fame, and is named for the 18th century actor David Garrick.

In the early 20th century the theatre was under the stewardship of the actor-manager Arthur Bourchier (1863-1927). The *Times* had this to say about his acting style:

"Never a great actor, he was nevertheless always a conspicuous figure in the theatrical world. He brought to his work an enthusiasm for the stage which gave to performances not artistically distinguished a curious effect of personal distinction... Sometimes his interpretations seemed to be misguided and his methods extravagantly theatrical, but here at least was an actor who was never colourless and, therefore, seldom dull."

Another critic, commenting on his appearance in *Macbeth*, said "Even murder cannot be as serious as all that," whilst another commentator observed of Bourchier's *Hamlet*: "At last we can settle whether Bacon or Shakespeare wrote the plays. Have the coffins opened and whichever has turned in his grave is the author."

Needless to say, Bourchier was not particularly enamoured of critics, and he made his mark on Theatreland when, in 1903, he point-blank refused to admit the drama critic of the *Times* into the theatre!

Despite the fact he moved on from The Garrick in 1915, his ghost still makes occasional returns to the building, and has been seen backstage during performances, as well as on the aptly named 'Phantom Staircase'. So why not stand outside, criticise one of his performances in a loud voice, and see if you don't incur his spectral wrath?

Incidentally, another of Bourchier's pet hates was cinema, so the fact that in the film *Batman Begins*, the scene in which young Bruce Wayne watches an opera with his parents was filmed here, night not sit too well with his wraith.

Continue along Charing Cross Road, and at the next traffic lights cross the road towards the National Portrait Gallery. Turn left on the other side, keep straight, and veer right into Trafalgar Square, keeping ahead past the columned portico of the National Galley. Having passed through Trafalgar Square, keep ahead over Whitcomb Street into Pall Mall East, go next right along Suffolk Street, and walk to its far end to pause outside Number 18 on the left and look up at the large window with the black balcony. This is the back of

Arthur Bourchier as Macbeth in 1910

11. THE THEATRE ROYAL, HAYMARKET

Built in 1720, this is the third-oldest London playhouse still in use. For a long period in the 19th century the theatre was managed by John Baldwin Buckstone (1802-1879), who was so fond of this theatre that he was never going to let a little thing like death prevent him from returning to the building he devoted so much of his life to.

Indeed, within a year of his death in 1879 his ghost was seen sitting in the Royal box, intently watching a performance.

It was on the staircase behind the window up at which you are looking that the late Sir Donald Sinden (1923-2014) encountered Buckstone's ghost whilst playing in *The Heiress* with Sir Ralph Richardson (1902-1983).

One night, Sir Donald and fellow performer Gill Cadell were coming down the staircase on their way to the stage when they passed a man in an old-fashioned dark suit, who had his back to them, and who was looking out of the window into Suffolk Street. Since Ralph Richardson's dressing room was on this floor they presumed it was him, and greeted him with "Good evening, Ralph."

The man made no reply, and, presuming that he was memorising his lines, they continued on their way down the stairs. On arrival at the next level, it

John Baldwin Buckstone

suddenly dawned on them that Richardson should have been on stage, so they hurried back up, only to find that the figure had now gone, and there was no sign of him anywhere.

In 2009, during a performance of *Waiting For Godot* at the theatre, Sir Patrick Stewart, came off stage during the interval and informed his co-star, Sir Ian McKellen, "I just saw a ghost on stage." Sir Ian was, according to Nigel Everett, a director at the theatre, "...stunned. I would not say frightened, but I would say impressed."

Linger as long as you dare, and then backtrack along Suffolk Street to turn right along Suffolk Place. Pause on the corner to look across the road at

12. HER MAJESTY'S THEATRE

Built by the actor and manager Sir Herbert Beerbohm-Tree (1852-1917), founder of the Royal Academy of Dramatic Art (RADA) and grandfather to the hell-raising actor Oliver Reed, Her Majesty's was completed in 1897, and was not just his place of work, but also his residence until his death in 1917. Indeed, the rather splendid, central, square French-style dome that sits atop the theatre was built for his personal use, containing a banqueting hall and living room.

He had a penchant for watching performances from the top box to the right of the stage, where modern audience members are said to have been alarmed by sudden drops in temperature from time to time, not to mention the door swinging open of its own accord.

Fittingly, the theatre was, from 1986 to 2020, the home to *Phantom of the Opera*.

Go left along Haymarket, veer right to cross the traffic light crossing at its end, keep ahead into Pall Mall and immediately cross the road via the crossing just before the red phone box. Turn right on the other side, and go left into Waterloo Place, proceeding clockwise around it, to pause by the railings just past the soaring Duke of York's Column. Behind the railings you will see a small gravestone.

---

13. GIRO'S GRAVESTONE

'Giro' Ein Truer Begleiter! London Im Februar 1934. Hoesch. This translates as, "'Giro' A faithful companion! London in February 1934. Hoesch."

The memorial remembers a German ambassador's

dog, and it is here because the building that stands to the right of the soaring tree that overshadows the tiny stone, 9 Carlton House Terrace, was the German Embassy until September 1939.

In consequence, the Giro memorial is often described, unfairly as it happens, as the only Nazi monument in London.

The German Ambassador in question was Leopold von Hoesch (1881-1936), who arrived in London on Wednesday, 2nd November 1932 to represent the Weimar Republic in Britain.

He had formerly been the German Ambassador to

Paris, and, upon his arrival in London, the British newspapers were fulsome in their praise of his diplomatic talents.

In addition to being an extremely able diplomat, he was also, according to the *Scotsman*, "Socially extremely popular." The newspaper went on to explain to its readers that,

"Herr von Hoesch is a bachelor, and, at all official banquets and receptions at the Paris Embassy, always did the honours himself unaided by any female relative or the wife of any of his secretaries..."

His diplomatic skills would be severely tested when, within a few months of his arrival, the Third Reich came to power in Germany, in January, 1933, and Herr von Hoesch found himself serving new and very different masters.

However, he rose to the challenge and became well-liked and admired by the majority of British politicians, who viewed him as a knowledgeable and able-minded statesman.

Over the next three years, he worked tirelessly to enhance Anglo-German relations.

When he took up residence at 9 Carlton House Terrace, in November, 1932, he brought with him to the Embassy his pet dog Giro, a German Shepherd – or at least that's what the majority of accounts say the dog's breed was.

The truth is, nobody actually knows that much about Giro. The only certainty is that he died in February 1934, and that is only certain because it is etched onto his gravestone.

As to how he died... Well, again, we don't really know; we just know that he must have died, because if he wasn't dead and they buried him in the Embassy garden... well, that's too cruel to contemplate!

Tradition maintains that the poor pooch was electrocuted when he chewed through an electric cable at the Embassy, but there is no actual proof of this being the case.

So, let's just say that Giro died in February 1934, and Herr von Hoesch had him buried in the Embassy garden, and commissioned the tiny tombstone on which he had carved the rather poignant inscription, *"Ein Truer Begleiter."*

Two years later, on Friday, 10th April 1936, at a little after 10.00am, von Hoesch was dressing after having had a bath in an apartment at the German Embassy, when he suffered a heart attack from which he died before medical aid could be summoned.

According to an Embassy official, who was quoted in the newspapers, his death was "so unexpected as to completely stun us all... Herr von Hoesch was thought to be in excellent health."

His death was generally attributed to the strain he had been under in trying to preserve Anglo-German relations, and it is perhaps no coincidence that shortly before his death, Joachim von Ribbentrop, Hitler's "Ambassador-at-Large", had paid a visit to London to represent Germany before the Council of the League of Nations.

With the outbreak of the Second World War, the German Embassy was closed and, after the war, the building was handed over to the Foreign Office until, in 1967, the current occupants, the Royal Society, moved in.

In 1966 an underground car park had been excavated on the strip of land between 9 Carlton Terrace and the Duke of York's steps.

It appears that Giro's tombstone was rediscovered, or at least noticed, during this building work, and it was moved to a new position in front of the tree, where it can now be seen by any passer-by who takes the trouble to peer through the gates in front of it.

....

Go down the steps to the left and keep ahead to turn right along The Mall. Keep ahead until you reach the corner of Marlborough Road and turn right along it, crossing to its left side and pausing by the open courtyard of

---

14. ST JAMES'S PALACE

Built by Henry VIII, St James's Palace remained one of the principle residences of the Kings and Queens of England for more than three hundred years. Its most famous haunting, however, dates from the first half of the 19th century.

In the early hours of 31st May 1810, Ernest Augustus, Duke of Cumberland and brother to George IV and William IV, was awoken from a deep sleep at around 2.30am, by what he at first though was a bat fluttering around his chamber.

The next thing he knew, he was subjected to a ferocious attack, as a sharp-bladed weapon began slashing at his padded nightcap and gown. As he attempted to deflect the blows, his hands and wrists were cut, and in desperation he screamed for help. A valet by the name of Cornelius Neale rushed to assist, and found the Duke's regimental sabre, covered in blood, lying on the floor by the door.

A doctor was summoned and, as his wounds were being treated, Cumberland asked for his other valet, Joseph Sellis, to be sent for. Two servants went to rouse him, but as they approached his room, they were startled by a strange gurgling sound from within.

Opening the door, they found Sellis lying dead on his bed. His throat had been cut back to the spine, and his head almost severed from his body. A hastily-convened inquest concluded that the dead valet had, for reasons unknown, attempted to murder his master, and in remorse had returned to his room to commit suicide.

Court gossip, however, had a different take on the matter, and talk of a cover-up was rife. Some said that Cumberland had, in fact, murdered Sellis, and pointed out that Sellis's hands were found to be clean and that there was bloodstained water in his wash-basin.

Would the valet, the doubters wondered, have had the time or the inclination to wash his hands, having, apparently, almost cut his own head off?

Several alternative scenarios were soon circulating as to what had really happened. One version maintained that Sellis had found the Duke in bed with his wife and, in an ensuing struggle, had been killed to stop him exposing Cumberland's adultery; another held that Cumberland had seduced Sellis's daughter who, finding herself with child, had committed suicide. When Sellis confronted his employer, the Duke had silenced him forever to avert a scandal.

Edgar's Guide To...

Satirical cartoon showing Duke of Cumberland being attacked by a wild-looking Sellis, his valet. The caption reads: "The Blessed effects of prefering (sic) Foreign Servants to our own Country Men." © The Trustees of the British Museum

In the mid-19th century an even wilder theory had it that the Duke and his other valet, Neale, were involved in "the grossest and most unnatural immorality," and that Sellis, having caught them in the act, was murdered on the Duke's orders.

Whatever the truth, there are occasions, when the old palace has settled at night, that the ghost of Sellis has been seen walking the corridors, a gaping wound across his throat, the sickly-sweet smell of fresh blood trailing in his spectral wake.

....

👉 *Keep ahead along Marlborough Road, pass through the covered passageway, turn left along Pall Mall, walk past the magnificent Tudor Gatehouse of St James's Palace, and keep ahead into Cleveland Row. Pause by the white building with the black balcony ahead, and look left to view, on the left, Clarence House, the London home of Prince Charles. Just be cautious here, as the barrier is guarded by two armed police officers, which can be a little disconcerting!*

....

15. THE PHANTOM OF CLARENCE HOUSE

Built in 1825 for the Duke of Clarence, who was later to become King William IV, Clarence House today is the London home of Prince Charles.

During World War II, the building housed the offices of the Foreign Relations Department of the British Red Cross Society.

In her book *Haunted Royal Homes*, Joan Forman tells of a clerk, Sonia Marsh, who was working alone in the vast building one Saturday afternoon when she got the uneasy feeling that something was watching her. Looking into the darkness, she saw a greyish, smoky, triangular mass coming towards her in a bobbing motion. Petrified, she leapt to her feet, grabbed her coat and raced from the building into the chill of a gloomy October afternoon.

When on Monday morning she told a colleague of her experience, the woman commented, 'It was probably the Old Duke of Connaught."

Arthur, Duke of Connaught, the third son of Queen Victoria, lived at Clarence House from 1900 until his death in 1942. It would appear, however, that his ghost was roaming the corridors and rooms of his London home for several years afterwards.

Pass to the right of the white building with the black balcony, and keep ahead along Cleveland Row, turn right on arrival at Stornaway House, and, on arrival at the railings, turn left through the gates of Milkmaid's Passage, turning right along Queen's Walk, and pause on the left to look into

---

16. GREEN PARK

The park is reputed to have been the burial ground for the nearby leper's hospital of St James's, and it cited as the reason for its lack of flowers.

Park-keepers whisper in hushed tones about a

*Arthur, Duke of Connaught:
the phantom of Clarence House?*

particular tree, which they have dubbed, rather poetically the 'Tree of Death'. They give it a wide berth when working in the park; no birds sing from its branches, and dogs avoid it. A general feeling of melancholy is said to emanate from it, which may account for the high number of suicides that have been found hanging from its branches.

A few witnesses have been scared witless by a throaty, gurgling chuckle that suddenly sounds from inside the tree. Others have caught glimpses of a tall, shadowy figure that stands beside it, pointing at them, but which vanishes the moment any brave or curious person moves towards it.

Since no-one really seems to know which tree is *the* tree, why not play a little came of Hunt the Tree of Death, and decide amongst yourselves which one you feel has the most sinister and melancholy feel about it?

....

Continue along Queen's Walk where, some way along on the right, you will find a very dark, narrow and almost sinister passage that passes under the buildings. Go through it, if you dare (and do keep in mind its gate closes at 10.00pm), and if you arrive at its other side, turn left, and then swing right into another narrow court to pause outside the yellow-painted house on the left.

17. SISTER ANN'S RETURN

For many years of the 19th century, this was the home of two spinster sisters, Ann and Harriet Pearson, who were deeply devoted to each other.

After Ann died, in 1858, Harriet lived in the house alone. But in November 1864, while on a visit to Brighton, she fell seriously ill. She was brought back to her London home and nursed by her two nieces, Mrs Coppinger and Miss Emma Pearson, and her

The St James's Place home of Ann and Harriet Pearson

nephew's wife, Mrs John Pearson.

On 23rd December heavy snow began to fall in the street outside, and a thick mist swirled around the windows of the house. Mrs Coppinger and Miss Pearson retired to bed, leaving Mrs Pearson to look after their ailing aunt. They left their door open and the landing gaslight burning.

At about one in the morning both jerked awake and saw their dead Aunt Ann go past their open door and into the sick room. Mrs Pearson then rushed into their room in a state of great agitation, having also seen and recognised the dead woman. All three returned to their aunt's bedside, where she told them that she had just seen her sister, and knew Ann had come to call her away.

Shortly afterwards, Aunt Harriet slipped into a coma, dying peacefully at 6 o'clock that evening.

....

Backtrack, go left along St James's Place, follow it as it swings left, and at its end turn left along St James's Street. On arrival at its top, cross over Piccadilly, go left on its other side, and turn right along Berkeley Street. Follow its entire length, then go left and walk clockwise around Berkeley Square. Having passed over the two crossings, you arrive on the left at

18. NUMBER 50 BERKELEY SQUARE

The plain Georgian exterior of 50 Berkeley Square belies an interior that still retains much of its 18th century grandeur. Sweeping stairs, high plaster ceilings, over-mantle mirrors, and marble floors and fireplaces, lend the building a decidedly Dickensian air. The house was once plagued by happenings so terrifying that, for much of the 19th century had the unenviable reputation of being "the most haunted house in London."

Charles Harper, in *Haunted Houses*, published in 1907 stated that

"It seems that a Something or Other, very terrible indeed, haunts or did haunt a particular room. This unnamed Raw Head and Bloody Bones, or whatever it is, has been sufficiently awful to have caused the death, in convulsions, of at least two foolhardy persons who have dared to sleep in that chamber..."

One of them was a nobleman, who, scoffing at tales that a hideous entity was residing within the haunted room, vowed to spend the night there. It was agreed, however, that should he require assistance he would ring the servants' bell to summon his friends.

So saying, he retired for the night. A little after midnight there was a faint ring, which was followed by a ferocious peeling of the bell. Rushing upstairs, the friends threw open the door, and found their companion, rigid with terror, his eyes bulging from their sockets.

He was unable to tell them what he had seen, and, such was the shock to his system, that he died shortly afterwards.

As a result of its dreadful reputation, no tenant could be found who was willing to take on the lease of 'the house' in Berkeley Square, and for many years it remained empty.

But its other-worldly inhabitants continued to be active. Strange lights that flashed in the windows would startle passers-by; disembodied screams were heard echoing from the depths of the building; and spookier still, the sound was heard of a heavy body being dragged down the staircase.

One night, two sailors on shore leave in London, were seeking a place to stay, chanced upon the obviously empty house. Breaking in, they made their way upstairs, and inadvertently settled down to spend the night in the haunted room.

They were woken by the sound of heavy, determined footsteps coming up the stairs. Suddenly the door banged open, and a hideous, shapeless, oozing mass began to fill the room. One sailor managed to get past it and escape.

THE "HAUNTED HOUSE," BERKELEY SQUARE

Returning to the house with a policeman, he found his friend's corpse, impaled on the railings outside, the twisted face and bulging eyes grim testimony to the terror that had caused him to jump to his death, rather than confront the evil in the room above.

Many theories have been put forward to account for the haunting of 50 Berkeley Square. Charles Harper reported that the house had once belonged to a Mr Du Pre of Wilton Park, who locked his lunatic brother in one of the attics.

The captive was so violent that he could only be fed through a hole, and his groans and cries could be heard in the neighbouring houses. When the brother died, his spectre remained behind to chill the blood and turn the mind of anyone unfortunate enough to encounter it.

Another hypothesis holds that a Mr Myers, who was engaged to a society beauty, once owned the house. He had set about furnishing the building in preparation for their new life together when, on the day of the wedding, his fiancé jilted him.

The disappointment undermined his reason, turning him into a bitter recluse. He locked himself away in the upstairs room and only came out at night to wander the house by flickering candlelight. It was these nocturnal ramblings that, so the theory goes,

gave the house its haunted reputation.

Whatever the events, tragic or otherwise, that lie behind the haunting of 50 Berkeley Square, there is no doubt that the building has a definite atmosphere about it.

Indeed, it is said that the fabric is so charged with psychic energy that merely touching the external brickwork can give a mild shock to the psychically inclined.

Nor are the ghosts, as is often claimed, consigned to

the buildings past. Julian Wilson, a bookseller with Maggs Brothers, was working alone in the accounts department which until recently occupied the haunted room, one Saturday morning in 2001, when a column of brown mist moved quickly across the room and vanished.

That same year a cleaner, preparing the house for a party, felt the overwhelming sensation that someone, or something, was standing behind her. Turning round she found that the room was empty. A man walking up the stairs was shocked when his glasses were snatched from his hand and flung to the ground.

In October 2001 I was asked to appear in a BBC documentary on *Haunted London*, and we were fortunate enough to be able to film inside 50 Berkeley Square.

Part of the programme entailed the soundman and myself having to stand in the dark in the haunted room for about five minutes, waiting for the signal to switch the lights on and off.

Although nothing actually happened, I can honestly say that I found it a truly frightening experience, and we were both glad to be able to rejoin the rest of the crew in the street outside.

☞ *If you dare, turn your back on the door of No. 50 and head right, to retrace your steps around Berkeley Square and then take the turning on your right onto Berkeley Street. Follow the road all the way to its end, where Piccadilly crosses. In front of you, to the left, is the Ritz Hotel, where former Prime Minister Margaret Thatcher died in 2013 – thankfully, she is yet to make a re-appearance – and to your right is Green Park Underground Station, where the Haunted West End walk ends.*

I wish you a pleasant remainder of your day, or night; get home safely, and when you retire to your beds later, do have sweet and pleasant dreams, and take care to remember that the scratching under your bed is but a figment of your imagination!

Pip, pip!

Edgar

REAL GHOST STORIES

No. — BERKELEY SQUARE, W.
by Elliott O'Donnell

Elliott O'Donnell (1872-1965) was a prolific author of ghost stories, with more than forty supernatural titles to his name. Travelling the world in search of spectres, it is possible that O'Donnell amassed the largest collection of spooky stories in history. The following article, which describes his meeting with a man who had spent a night in the haunted house in Berkeley Square, and his own subsequent visit, appeared in *The Tatler* of 8th September 1909.

*

The other day I received a letter from a gentleman greatly interested in my recent work, *Some Haunted Houses of England and Wales*. Of course I consented to an interview; it is always interesting to meet people who have had actual encounters with the superphysical, and I went to the Hotel Roland where he was staying.

"I have only encountered the super-physical once,"

he said; "it appalled me. I cannot efface it from my memory. Another such ordeal would kill me.

"The incident took place three years ago; my companion was a doctor, Leslie Merrick. We had both been very anxious to investigate the hauntings in Berkeley Square and were delighted beyond measure when the owner of No.-- invited us to spend a night there.

"We had set apart the evening of November 5 for our enterprise and arrived at the house about eight o'clock. Neither of us had any idea as to the nature of the hauntings, nor did we for one moment think the phenomena could be other than phantasms of the dead; we had no notion of any other type of ghost. We explored the gloomy house from top to bottom, eventually deciding to spend the night in a large back bedroom which we both agreed was the most likely-looking spot for a ghostly visitation. We made ourselves as comfortable as the circumstances permitted, Merrick selecting the bed – a tremendous old four-poster – for his post of observation, and I an ottoman at the foot of it.

"We shut the door and waited. Every now and then the hush was broken by one of those ominous creakings that so often arouse one's attention in the depth of the night and are so strangely unaccountable.

"Once I thought I heard the handle of a door gently turned and once the light in Merrick's hand wavered, and once again – but there, our nerves were in such a state of tension that the most trivial noise might easily have passed for a Brobdingnagian bellow.

"The atmosphere grew steadily colder as the night advanced. At midnight it must have been freezing.

"An irrepressible tremor now pervaded my frame. I felt sure we were no longer alone in the house but that something – something, Mr. O'Donnell, to which I could not assign a name – had suddenly and surreptitiously entered the lower premises.

"I glanced at Merrick; the lantern was shaking in his hand, his face was ghastly. I did not speak to him – I wanted, I even longed, to do so – but I dared not; I was afraid of my own voice.

"Overpowered by this intense feeling of horror, augmented if anything by the presence of Merrick, whose alarm was inconceivably terrifying, I was compelled to keep my seat and wait.

"Out of the indefinable there at length developed something definite – a sound on the staircase, soft, heavy, and suggestive of a crawling horror.

"It ascended slowly nearer and nearer. I felt obliged to look at Merrick. His lantern was fully turned on the door; it no longer shook. He had controlled his agitation by a mighty effort, but his eyes were dreadful.

"The soft tread reached the top stair; it crossed the landing, it halted outside our door, the handle turned – I swear I saw it turn – and the Thing entered.

"I did not see it, I could not see it. I was afraid to look.

"I heard it approach Merrick – tread, tread, tread – across the soft carpet towards the bed.

"Merrick saw it, and as I looked at him my blood froze. I can't get his face out of my mind; it haunts me now. The terror in it was appalling, hellish, damnable. It was not Merrick; it was the Thing he saw, it was reflected in his countenance – he was a blurred edition of it.

"I watched his mouth open; I knew he was endeavouring to shriek for help. I understood his inability to do so.

"The Thing crawled up to him. He tried to beat it off; it wriggled on to the bed, it squirmed over him, it came for me. I fled. God forgive me, Mr. O'Donnell – I fled.

"A policeman was at hand. I told him, and we entered the house together.

"Merrick was lying face downwards on the bed insensible. The Thing had gone. No, he didn't die –

at least, not just then, Mr. O'Donnell, but he lost his reason and a few months later developed internal cancer which proved fatal. I have since learned that other people who either lived in that house or merely visited it died of the same disease."

"Sarcoma."

I obtained leave, and a week after my interview with him I visited No.-- Berkeley Square, accompanied by a cat – a big comfortable-looking black cat.

It was August 11. The night was light, the weather warm, and pussy soon settled herself snugly down on the bed which had proved so fatal a resting place to poor Merrick.

Ten o'clock struck; a red glow stealing through the window pane illuminated the carpet.

Eleven, half-past eleven o'clock, struck, then silence – a silence that intensified as midnight drew nearer.

I was now assailed for the first time with fear – fear that might probably be accounted for, in part at least, by the story of the unfortunate Merrick.

I had done something cruel – I had fastened poor pussy to the bed. She was there as an experiment. Cats are susceptible both to the superphysical and to sarcoma.

The house was deadly still; its heavy, sombre furniture

smothered every sound. I struggled to reason off the nervousness which was gradually gaining dominion over me, but my efforts were fruitless, and as the clock struck twelve I was convulsed with a paroxysm of the most unaccountable, ungovernable terror.

A soft tread crossed the hall and began to ascend the stairs.

Overpowered by my feelings I now sprang to my feet and pushing a chair in front of me prepared for the worst.

Up, up, up, four more steps – three, two, one. The landing, half- way across, the door, my door. My God, it is entering! What is it? Oh what is it?

I looked at pussy; she had sprung to her feet in the greatest state of agitation, her hair bristling on end, her mouth wide open, her eyes all pupil.

I am psychic. Ghosts invariably show themselves to me, and I saw this one.

What it was I cannot exactly say save that it resembled a small man with a large head, bloated, distorted features, and eyes which defy description. They were larger and fuller than those of a human being – yellowish green and wholly bestial. The mouth was merely a jagged slit. The head was covered with a mass of matted tow-coloured hair; there were no ears. Its body was nude – green, pulpy, unwholesome, beastly.

THE GHOST OF BERKELEY SQUARE

Drawn by the author shortly after an encounter with this fearsome apparition

More I cannot say saving that it crawled on all fours and had two additional arms – or what resembled arms – instead of legs.

It fixed its hideous gaze on the bed and crawled towards it.

The cat grew frantic. Again and again it essayed to break the bonds with which I had so securely tied it to the bed. It mewed, it screamed, it foamed, it tore the air wildly with its claws, and as two loathsome hands closed over it it fell on its back and fought.

Now was my opportunity, my only chance. A minute more and the phantasm would turn its attention to me.

I darted round the bed; I rushed at the door, I tore it open, and from that cursed cancer-stricken house I lied for dear life.

*

I

I live in a house with no windows
a black curtain hangs on my door.
The voices of conscience torment me
I live in a room with no floor.

II

There's dirt in the corner I can't see
there's water that runs down the wall.
There're mice in the attic above me
and rats playing games in the hall.

III

I live in a house with no windows~
and sleep in a room with no heat.
The darkness of life that surrounds me
Keeps out the sounds of the street.

IV

I wake when the shadows have fallen
and walk when the memories cease.
When purpose in life has no meaning
and only the wicked find peace.

V

Each night you sense that I'm by you
you feel my breath as you sleep.
You hear the faint creak of the floorboards
as out from the shadows I creep.

VI

I live in a house with no windows
I live in a house that's now yours
It's my voice you think that you're hearing
for I died in this room with no doors.

© (1997) Richard Jones
All rights reserved.

www.ingramcontent.com/pod-product-compliance
Lightning Source LLC
Chambersburg PA
CBHW021950160426
43195CB00011B/1311